The Great Ends of the Church

Writer: Joseph D. Small

Published especially for use in the Presbyterian Church (U.S.A.), by CMP, a ministry of the Presbyterian Mission Agency, Presbyterian Church (U.S.A.), Louisville, Kentucky.

Printed in the U.S.A.

Writer:
Joseph D. Small served as director of the Presbyterian Church (U.S.A.) Office of Theology and Worship from 1989–2011. He is now adjunct faculty at the University of Dubuque Theological Seminary and church relations consultant to the Presbyterian Foundation. He serves on the board of the Center for Catholic and Evangelical Theology, the Faith and Order Commission of the National Council of the Churches of Christ in the USA, and is co-chair of the international Reformed-Pentecostal Dialogue. He participates in international ecumenical consultations sponsored by the World Council of Churches, the World Communion of Reformed Churches, and the Centre International Réformé. Dr. Small is the author of *To Be Reformed: Living the Tradition* (2010), *Let Us Reason Together: Christians and Jews in Conversation* (2010), *Proclaiming the Great Ends of the Church* (2010), and several other books, articles, and monographs. He is married to Valerie Small, a Presbyterian ruling elder who serves as an assistant stated clerk of the General Assembly. They are the parents of four children: Kalen, Doug, Jennifer, and Carly.

Editor:
Donald K. McKim is editor for *Being Reformed: Faith Seeking Understanding,* the adult curriculum of the Presbyterian Church (U.S.A.). He also serves as editor of *These Days*. Dr. McKim is an honorably retired Presbyterian minister who has been an editor for Westminster John Knox Press, a seminary theology professor, an academic dean, and a pastor. He is the author and editor of a number of books on Reformed theology, including *Introducing the Reformed Faith; Presbyterian Beliefs: A Brief Introduction; Presbyterian Questions, Presbyterian Answers; More Presbyterian Questions, More Presbyterian Answers,* and the *Westminster Handbook to Reformed Theology*. He lives with his wife, LindaJo McKim, in Germantown, Tennessee. They have two married children and two grandchildren.

Contents

The Great Ends of the Church

Introduction to *Being Reformed: Faith Seeking Understanding*

Reformed and Presbyterian Christians are people of faith who are seeking understanding. From the beginnings of our Reformed tradition, Presbyterians have realized God calls us to explore ways the Christian faith can be more fully known and expressed. This vision has driven concerns for the education of people of all ages. Presbyterians have been big on providing resources to help us delve more deeply into Christian faith and the theology that gives our living tradition its distinctive heritage.

This *Being Reformed* curriculum for adults is one expression of the desire to open up what it means to be Presbyterian Christians in the world today. Our purpose is to enhance, enrich, and expand our insights. We want Presbyterians to grow in understandings of elements that are foundational and significant for their faith. Encounters with theology, church, worship, spirituality/discipleship, and social righteousness will guide our ways.

These studies engage our whole selves. We will find our minds moved by new ideas, our emotions stirred with responses of gratitude, and calls for action that can lead us in different life directions. Heads, hearts, and hands will be drawn into the joys of discovering what new things God is calling us toward.

We invite you to join this journey of faith seeking understanding. Celebrate the blessings of our Reformed and Presbyterian tradition of faith. Be stimulated and challenged by fresh insights that will deepen your understandings. Find a stronger commitment to the God who has loved us in Jesus Christ.

Introduction to *The Great Ends of the Church*

One of the treasures of the Presbyterian Church (U.S.A.) is the great ends of the church. These six statements have provided guidance for the church as faithful expressions of the Christian gospel and as what God calls the church to be and do.

This excellent study will bring the great ends to life in significant ways for our denomination and for congregations. They challenge each of us to show and tell the gospel through God's church.

Under expert guidance here, the six great ends are examined in a helpful pairing of one with another. This enables us to see the emphases and the balances the church needs to reflect as it lives out the purposes for which the triune God establishes it. When the church knows its theological groundings, it can follow the lead of the Holy Spirit in witnessing to the gospel of Jesus Christ in word and deed.

The six great ends are to be taken as a whole. The fullness of the gospel is expressed as the church witnesses to the different dimensions toward which the great ends point us. The church's ministries—and our own—are energized when we realize ways the gospel can be lived out.

This study leads us to rejoice: "through the church the wisdom of God in its rich variety might now be made known" (Ephesians 3:10)!

Donald K. McKim

Mission Statements

Scripture

2 Corinthians 5:14–21 The church does not live for itself, but for Christ.

Prayer

Holy God: you have chosen us to serve you, and appointed us the agents of your love. We thank you for prophets who recall us to your will. We are grateful for every impulse to confess and correct wrongs, to keep faith pure and purposes faithful. We praise you for your Holy Spirit always reforming the church, so we may better serve as disciples of your Son, Jesus Christ the Lord. Amen.[1]

Introduction

Mission statements—every organization seems to have one. Grocery chains, oil producers, pharmaceutical companies, and social networking services all devise pithy statements designed to communicate their noble purpose and efficient service. Christian congregations are no exception. We regularly adopt brief mission statements describing who we are, communicating a vibrant vision of faith and action. Our congregational self-descriptions are usually abstract idealizations, possibly intended more in hope than as actual depiction. Perhaps that is why they are so easily forgotten.

For more than a half century, the Presbyterian Church (U.S.A.) has embedded a brief mission statement in its *Book of Order*. An inventory of the great ends of the church, first articulated in 1910 by one of the PC(USA)'s predecessor denominations—the United Presbyterian Church of North America—was incorporated into the denominational unions of 1958 and 1983.

1. *The Worshipbook* (Philadelphia: The Westminster Press, 1970), 161. Used with permission.

The great ends of the church are:

> the proclamation of the gospel for the salvation of humankind;
> the shelter, nurture, and spiritual fellowship of the children of God;
> the maintenance of divine worship;
> the preservation of the truth;
> the promotion of social righteousness; and
> the exhibition of the Kingdom of Heaven to the world.[2]

The great ends of the church is not a typical mission statement. Instead of setting out an idealized description of who we are, it challenges us by telling us who *we are to be*. With an economy of words and a surplus of meaning, these six great purposes of the church's life compose a genuine Presbyterian mission statement. They set before us six foundational works of the church that express who and what the church is called to be and how the church is called to act. They are not included in the *Book of Order* as taken-for-granted assumptions about ourselves, but as the calling of each congregation, every presbytery, and the whole General Assembly and all its agencies. Why, then, do congregations, presbyteries, and the General Assembly spend so much time and effort on disconnected, manufactured, and constantly revised visions, mission statements, and goals?

Everything Grows Together

The great ends of the church is not a list of disconnected items, but a holistic vision of the church's life. The church cannot be faithful to the intention of the great ends by emphasizing some while neglecting others. These basic purposes of the church do not allow us to stress proclamation of the gospel while neglecting nurture within the congregation, or to promote social righteousness while failing to guard the truth of Christian doctrine. The great purposes of the church are intimately related to one another; none can be fully understood apart from its relation to each of the others and to the whole.

Yet too many congregations and denominations regularly fall into the practice of limiting their efforts by emphasizing social engagement to the neglect of faithful worship, for example, or stressing doctrine at the expense of joyful proclamation. Lopsided

2. Presbyterian Church (U.S.A.), *Book of Order 2013–2015* (Louisville, KY: Office of the General Assembly, 2013), F-1.0304.

priorities are rarely intentional. More often than not, we fall into constricted patterns of church life without noticing what we have lost. We may play to our real or imagined strengths rather than face weaknesses honestly. We may allow some useful structures or successful programs to crowd out other aspects of faithful church life. We simply may become content with the way things are, thereby missing a vision of the way things could and should be. The great ends of the church offers a needed corrective, a comprehensive check-up that provides us with a faithful way to examine our life together.

The great ends of the church offers a needed corrective, a comprehensive check-up that provides us with a faithful way to examine our life together.

The interconnectedness of the church's six foundational purposes becomes evident in an intriguing way when they are paired from the inside out.

- "Maintenance of divine worship" *and* "preservation of the truth." There is no separation between devotion and integrity, drama and doctrine, beauty and truth. Worship that neglects the truth of the gospel—no matter how engaging, creative, and inspiring it may be—does not maintain the worship of God. Truth without praise and prayer is not the truth about God. The great ends of the church display their unity.
- "Shelter, nurture, and spiritual fellowship of the children of God" *and* "promotion of social righteousness." There should be no tension between the internal life and outward mission of the church. Focus on the inner life of a congregation or denomination without active engagement in the quest for social justice leads to self-seeking introversion, while focus on social action apart from attention to the internal life of the faith community leads to centrifugal exhaustion. The great ends of the church display their unity.
- "Proclamation of the gospel for the salvation of humankind" *and* "exhibition of the Kingdom of Heaven to the world." Senseless debates about verbal evangelism versus the witness of our lives are put aside when their mutuality becomes evident in the comprehensive design of the great ends. Speaking the gospel is oddly abstract without the witness of Christian life; the witness of Christian life without the gospel narrative is vague and ambiguous. The great ends of the church display their unity.

Bulletins and Banners?

The great ends of the church presents us with a unified vision of the church's purpose, and each of the six aims presents us with a sharp challenge concerning the ways we shape church life. Why, then, are the great ends so often ignored in favor of fabricated congregational and denominational mission statements? Why, when the great ends are used, are they routinely relegated to customary words in Sunday bulletins or artistic symbols on decorative banners? Presbyterians tend to be legalists about *Book of Order* rules and regulations, but the *Book of Order's* more theological and ethical affirmations are treated as window dressing, ecclesial ornaments admired and then disregarded.

> *The great ends of the church presents us with a unified vision of the church's purpose, and each of the six aims presents us with a sharp challenge concerning the ways we shape church life.*

There are multiple causes for our neglect of these six fundamental purposes of the church's life. Underlying all of them, however, may be their pointed specificity, both individually and as a whole.

- "Proclamation of the gospel for the salvation of humankind" has no room for glib, generalized references to the gospel. This great end specifies that the gospel of Christ's life, death, and resurrection is good news about the *salvation* of *humankind*. Furthermore, we are challenged to *proclaim* this gospel, not merely to believe it.
- "Shelter, nurture, and spiritual fellowship of the children of God" goes beyond comfortable congregational life to encompass *all* of God's children. Some need shelter from the *dangers* of violence or unemployment, most need nurture *in the faith,* and all need fellowship *in the Spirit* far beyond Sunday coffee hours.
- "Maintenance of divine worship" takes us beyond debates over worship styles—"traditional" or "contemporary"—to the realization that worship is not about us, but about our praise of the one God—Father, Son, and Holy Spirit—and our obedience to God's Word.
- "Preservation of the truth" means we are not at liberty to believe whatever we wish to believe, but the truth about God and ourselves must be taught, believed, lived, and sustained.

- "Promotion of social righteousness" makes clear that engaging God's justice in both church and society is not an optional feature of Christian faith and life, much less an unwelcome intrusion into "spiritual" religion.
- "Exhibition of the Kingdom of Heaven to the world" compels us to examine the character of our individual and corporate Christian life. When the world looks at us, what does it see? Does what it sees reflect God's new Way in the world, or does it simply mirror the way things already are in the world?

None of this is easy. It is more comfortable for some people, congregations, and even denominations to avoid one or more of these six challenges because they do not conform to existing convictions or preferences. "Promotion of social righteousness" may be dismissed as meddling in politics. "Proclamation of the gospel for the salvation of humankind" may be scorned as fundamentalism that fails to recognize the value of other faiths. We may find comfort in being satisfied with the existing shape of congregational worship or small-group fellowship, and so have no need for bothersome self-examination.

The Great Challenges to the Church

The great ends of the church present us with pointed challenges to our routine ways of thinking about the church's life, about its faith and its mission. They call us to bold declaration of the gospel, deep spiritual lives, reformed worship, fidelity to the truth, justice in the church and the world, and visible witness to Christ in our personal and ecclesial lives. The great ends also present us with challenging paths toward these purposes:

exhibit!
promote!
preserve!
maintain!
shelter and nurture!
proclaim!

The great ends spur us to action. They do not ask us to contemplate the nobility of their aims, but to commit ourselves to move toward their fulfillment.

The great ends spur us to action. They do not ask us to contemplate the nobility of their aims, but to commit ourselves to move toward their fulfillment.

No congregation is perfect or will ever be beyond reproach. No denomination is flawless, and all denominations live in perpetual deficiency. Our inevitable failure to achieve the church's great purposes should not discourage us from striving toward the faithful goals set before us, however. The six great ends are both the horizon toward which we are called to travel and directional signs along the way. They are a road map as well as a destination. They are gifts to us from our forebears, the result of their best thinking about the shape of the new life to which Christ calls us. They come to us as encouragements to our faithful living, not as indictments of our grand and petty failures.

The church's six purposes challenge us, setting out touchstones, beckoning us toward deeper love of God and neighbor. For that reason, they must never become standards we employ to critique others. If we use them to evaluate other congregations or to pass judgment on our denomination, we pervert their intent. Viewing others with contempt, saying, "God, I thank you that I am not like other people" (Luke 18:11), is as self-deceiving as it is censorious. The great ends of the church are the unified purposes for all Presbyterian congregations, every presbytery, and all national structures. However, while the whole church is called to fulfill these purposes, their challenge begins with us, where we are. Diverting their light away from us and toward others only succeeds in leaving us in darkness.

Church studies sometimes proceed in an atmosphere of detachment as the "subject" of the study is observed from a distance. As we continue this study of the great ends of the church, we will move beyond detachment to engagement. We may then be able to let these central purposes examine us, helping us discover how they can become aids to the continuing reformation of our church. They call us to renewed ecclesial and personal faithfulness. Our purpose in this study is not merely to learn *about* these central purposes of the church's life, but to understand how to use them as lenses that show us more clearly the realities of our church's life and the possibilities for its ongoing renewal.

Spiritual Practice

On six successive days, meditate for five minutes on the Scripture passage suggested for each of the great ends of the church:
1) proclamation of the gospel: Romans 10:14; 2) shelter, nurture, and spiritual fellowship: Acts 4:32–35; 3) worship: Psalm 150; 4) truth: John 1:14; 5) righteousness: Amos 5:24; 6) kingdom of heaven: Luke 13:18–19.

Questions for Reflection

If the great ends of the church are familiar to you, how did you learn about them? How were they used? If they are new to you, why do you think you haven't heard about them before?

Which of the six great purposes of the church most challenges you? Your congregation?

Would the great ends of the church be a suitable mission statement for your congregation? For the PC(USA)?

The Church

Scripture

1 Peter 2:9–10 We are what we are only because God has called us.

Prayer

Mighty God: you have called us together, and, by your Holy Spirit, made us one with your Son our Lord. We thank you for the church, for the power of the word and the sacraments. We praise you for apostles, martyrs, and brave people who have witnessed for you. We are glad you have joined us with believers throughout the world, and that you send us into the world full of the Holy Spirit to say that you are love; through Jesus Christ our Lord. Amen.[1]

Introduction

The great ends are the purposes of the church. What do we mean when we use the word *church?* Everyday speech encompasses a jumble of meanings: buildings, people, congregations, organizations, judicatories, and Christians everywhere. Unlike other languages, English does not make distinctions among realities as diverse as buildings and communities of faith, denominations, and global councils. Modest efforts have been made to overcome some English limitations, such as the once-common distinction between uppercase *Church* referring to the whole body of Christians across time and space and lowercase *church* referring to a specific ecclesial institution. Even this limited attempt at clarity has been largely discarded.

The problem is compounded by the now-common use of church to refer to non-Christian religious bodies. The Lutheran Church, the Catholic Church, and all other Christian churches often are thought to belong to the same genre as the Mormon "church," the "church" of Scientology, and even—according to a Louisville TV reporter—the Buddhist "church." In ordinary usage, *church* has

1. *The Worshipbook* (Philadelphia: The Westminster Press, 1970), 152, alt. Used with permission.

become synonymous with *religious institution*. This equation leads to a number of difficulties, not the least of which is thinking of the great ends of the church as management categories, as if their fulfillment is merely a matter of applying the latest organizational techniques.

Before dealing with the church's great purposes, it will help to be clear about what we mean by *church*. The New Testament word for "church," *ekklēsia,* signifies an assembly, a gathering of people summoned for a particular purpose. It is rooted in two words, *ek* ("from") and *kaleō* ("call"). The church is the assembly of people who have been called together. This is sometimes taken to mean the church is called out from the world and so must separate from worldly ways. However, the emphasis belongs elsewhere—on the caller, the One who summons, the triune God. The church is the assembly called by God through Christ in the power of the Holy Spirit. The church is not its own creation, and its purpose is not its own to devise.

The Assembly

Reformed thinking about the church begins with the conviction that the gathered congregation is the basic form of church. More precisely, a Reformed theology of the church understands the congregation is most truly itself when it is gathered around word, water, bread and wine, in worship of God-with-us (Emmanuel) whose active Word is spoken: "I will be your God, and you shall be my people" (Jeremiah 7:23).

It is also a basic conviction of Reformed ecclesiology that the gathered congregation is not a sufficient form of church. The congregation gathered by God through Word and sacrament *is* the one holy catholic and apostolic church, but not by itself alone. The gathered congregation is the one holy catholic and apostolic church only in its essential communion with the Lord and therefore its communion with other gathered congregations.

The sixteenth-century Reformation's approach to the nature and purpose of the church began, not with the church itself, but with Christ. In the words of the Ten Theses of Berne (1528), "The holy Christian Church, whose only head is Christ, is born of the Word of God, and abides in the same, and listens not to the voice of a stranger."[2] The church is called into being and is sustained by the Word of God, Jesus Christ. However, God's Word is not the only voice

2. "The Ten Conclusions of Berne," *Creeds of the Churches*, third edition, ed. John H. Leith (Louisville: John Knox Press, 1982), 129.

that beckons us, for the divine call sounds amid many other voices—cultural, societal, political, and religious. The true Word of God always calls the church back to its true self.

John Calvin (1509–1564) said we can recognize this creation of the Word, the church, "wherever we see the Word of God purely preached and heard, and the sacraments administered according to Christ's institution."[3] The clearest indicators of the one holy catholic and apostolic church are the proclamation of Jesus Christ together with baptism and the Lord's Supper celebrated in fidelity to Christ. They are clear indicators because they are the surest means of Christ's audible and visible presence with his people.

God's Word is not the only voice that beckons us, for the divine call sounds amid many other voices—cultural, societal, political, and religious. The true Word of God always calls the church back to its true self.

Word and sacraments are not the only things congregations do, of course. Congregations engage in a wide variety of missions, ministries, programs, and activities. However, church initiatives and services must not bury Word and sacrament or push them to the periphery of congregational and denominational life. The whole range of things the church does rightly grows from preaching and teaching, baptism and Eucharist, and is subject to authentication by Word and sacrament. They are not merely liturgical activities; they are the embodiment of the gospel in the life of Christ's people. The question to be asked of any congregation is whether Word and sacraments are found at the heart of its common life or simply confined to a Sunday routine.

Union with Christ

Each gathered congregation consists of people who have responded to God's gracious call in Jesus Christ. Human responses are never perfect; the congregation gathered around pulpit, font, and table is a blend of faithfulness and faithlessness, ebbing and flowing in time. Nevertheless, the One who calls is the ever-faithful, ever-present Christ, whose invitation comes in a gracious multitude of ways. People are not gathered by their devotion, but in their ambiguous response to Christ's call—some in gratitude and others in hope, some in service and others in need, some in anticipation and others

3. John Calvin, *Institutes of the Christian Religion,* trans. Ford Lewis Battles, ed. John T. McNeill, Library of Christian Classics (Philadelphia: The Westminster Press, 1960), 4.1.9 (1023).

out of habit. Responses to Christ's call cannot be clearly divided into pure and tainted. God alone knows our hearts; all we know is that the church is the *ekklēsia,* the called ones whose responses are mixed. Novelist John Updike portrays the church with remarkable insight when he notes, "A company of believers is like a prisonful of criminals: their intimacy and solidarity are based on what about themselves they can least justify."[4]

The church is not left to its own devices, however, reduced to self-deceptive celebration or self-defeating despair. Although our response to Christ's call is always ambiguous, Christ's call remains his faithful call to be joined to him in doing the will of God on earth as it is in heaven. The church is the place where Christ's call resounds most clearly. Present with us in Word and sacrament, Christ's call is not a distant summons but an intimate disclosure that we are his friends, his sisters and brothers, his body. The gathered congregation is most truly itself in full communion with its Savior and Lord.

"Union with Christ" has long been a hallmark of Reformed ecclesiology. "Christ," says Calvin, "having been made ours, makes us sharers with him in the gifts with which he has been endowed. We do not, therefore, contemplate him outside ourselves from afar . . . but because we put on Christ and are engrafted into his body—in short, because he deigns to make us one with him . . . we glory that we have communion of righteousness with him."[5] United with Christ as Christ has united himself to us, we enter into communion with the one God—Father, Son, and Holy Spirit. Union with Christ is not simply personal, although it is that. More fundamentally, union with Christ is an ecclesial reality. Our Lord still prays for us, "As you, Father, are in me and I am in you, may they also be in us . . . I in them and you in me, that they may become completely one" (John 17:21, 23). Christ's call continues to beckon us, prompting our reply and encouraging our growth as the body of Christ, that we may love God with heart, soul, mind, and strength and love all neighbors as ourselves.

Christ's call continues to beckon us, prompting our reply and encouraging our growth as the body of Christ, that we may love God with heart, soul, mind, and strength and love all neighbors as ourselves.

4. John Updike, *In the Beauty of the Lilies* (New York: Knopf, 1996), 416.
5. Calvin, *Institutes,* 3.11.10 (737).

A Communion of Congregations

We Presbyterians are fond of referring to ourselves as a "connectional church." Even with the best intentions, however, the term has an organizational, institutional ring; it suggests legislative and managerial church structures. Perhaps we should use a biblical term, *koinōnia,* to express the relationship among congregations. *Koinonia* is rendered in English translations as *communion, fellowship, participation, partnership, sharing, contribution,* and *taking part.* The variety of translations suggests the richness of the term, yet as we read the New Testament we are unaware that one Greek word underlies seemingly unrelated English terms, and we miss the astonishing range of contexts in which *koinōnia* is used.

Koinōnia expresses the most significant features of Christian faith and life: communion with the triune God; communion with others in faith, hope, and love; communion in sacraments; communion in the truth of the gospel; communion in faithful living; communion in the reconciliation of differences; communion in patterns of mutual responsibility and accountability.[6] All these elements are interrelated aspects of the deep, intimate, abiding mutuality that characterizes new relationships between God and us, among us as a congregation, and among congregations.

Some congregations nurture deep mutual relationships among their members, while others are more like gatherings of strangers. Relationships among Presbyterian congregations too often are confined to organizational links in presbyteries, synods, and the General Assembly. Church councils seldom bond congregations together in relationships of mutual responsibility and accountability to nurture communion among them. Instead, they meet to do business. Presbyterian "communion" through councils is vertical and managerial, not horizontal and relational.

How would we know genuine communion among congregations if we saw it? With a bow to Calvin, we might say that "a communion of congregations would come forth and become visible to our eyes wherever we could see the Word of God preached and taught and studied and heard and lived out in common, and the sacraments shared regularly and normally in accordance with Christ." Hearing

6. For a small sample of texts, see 1 John 1:1–3; 1 Corinthians 1:4–9; Acts 2:42–45; 1 Corinthians 10:16–17; 1 John 1:6–7; Philippians 2:1–5; Galatians 2:9; 2 Corinthians 9:13–14; Romans 15:25–27.

the Word of God together and praying with and for one another, congregations would grow in living the Word together, loving God, and loving the world God loves. United in baptism and Eucharist, congregations would live out their union with Christ sacramentally, dying to the old life of indifferent self-sufficiency and sitting with fellow sinners at Christ's table.

Hearing the Word of God together and praying with and for one another, congregations would grow in living the Word together, loving God, and loving the world God loves. United in baptism and Eucharist, congregations would live out their union with Christ sacramentally, dying to the old life of indifferent self-sufficiency and sitting with fellow sinners at Christ's table.

Communion among congregations would go far beyond thinking well of one another, instituting periodic pulpit exchanges, conducting joint vacation Bible schools, or establishing limited missional relationships. Communion would shape deep patterns of mutual responsibility and accountability, finding material expression in the generous sharing of resources. Sharing money was the issue at hand in the early church, and it is still a mark of communion's actuality. Yet communion in material resources is only one tangible verification of genuine *koinōnia* in sharing the full resources of congregational energy, intelligence, imagination, and love.

Spiritual Practice

Spend five to ten minutes meditating on Jeremiah 7:23: "I will be your God, and you shall be my people." Linger on each element: *I . . . your God . . . you . . . my people.* Conclude by praying several times, "You alone are our God, O Lord, and we together are your people, in Christ."

Questions for Reflection

Are proclamation (preaching and teaching) and sacraments (baptism and the Lord's Supper) at the heart of our congregation's life? Is one emphasized at the expense of the other?

How does our congregation's presbytery encourage communion among congregations?

How can our congregation explore possibilities for genuine communion with just one neighboring Presbyterian congregation?

Worship in Spirit and in Truth

Scripture

John 4:23 Worship and truth are inseparably linked.

Prayer

Holy God: you call us to worship, and by your Spirit prompt prayers and praise. Keep us from saying words or singing hymns with ritual disinterest. Fill us with such wonder that we may worship you, grateful for the mystery of your unfailing love for us, in Jesus Christ the Lord. Amen.[1]

Introduction

The six great ends of the church are interrelated parts in a unified description of faithful Christian life for every expression of the church. Treating each one separately runs the danger of imagining the great ends can be understood in isolation from one another. Our study of the church's foundational purposes will treat them in pairs before concluding with a holistic pairing of the *great ends* and the *church*.

Pairing the great ends follows naturally from their structure. This becomes clear when we begin from the outside in. In this way, "proclamation of the gospel for the salvation of *humankind*" is paired with "exhibition of the Kingdom of Heaven to *the world.*" Both are directed outward, toward the whole world and everyone in it, one in verbal proclamation and the other in visible witness. Taking the next step inward, we pair "shelter, nurture, and spiritual fellowship of the *children of God*" with "promotion of *social* righteousness." The life of the church and the life of society are inseparable. Then, at the heart of the church's great purposes, we find "maintenance of divine *worship*" and "preservation of the *truth.*" Praise without the truth about God and ourselves soon degenerates into deceptive self-affirmation; the truth about God

1. *The Worshipbook* (Philadelphia: The Westminster Press, 1970), 200. Used with permission.

and ourselves without praise and prayer evaporates into impersonal abstraction.

The three pairings not only are inherent in the structure of the great ends of the church; they also help prevent distortions that might result from viewing each purpose in isolation from the whole. The pairings are even more evocative of the full life of the church when they are understood from the inside out. The fullness of the gospel—the grace of the Lord Jesus Christ, the love of God, and the communion of the Holy Spirit—is the indispensable core of the church's faith and life. Without the true knowledge of God's Way in the world, the church will lurch from blunder to miscalculation in pursuit of its own ways, guided only by its own desires. Yet knowledge of the truth without grateful response of adoration and praise of God is barren—in fact, not truth at all.

What Is Truth?

On the day of his execution, Jesus declared that he came into the world to testify to the truth and that everyone who belongs to the truth listens to his voice. Pilate responded with his infamous question, "What is truth?" (John 18:38). Though we hear his question as cynical resignation, it is our question as well. How can we know what is true and what is false about everything from child rearing to retirement planning, from the claims of drug companies to the promises of politicians? Is there no certainty to be had, only different "truths" for different people? Is truth unattainable in the crowded field of preferences and opinions?

When we encounter Pilate's question in John's Gospel, we already know the answer. "And the Word became flesh and lived among us . . . full of grace and truth" (John 1:14); "grace and truth came through Jesus Christ" (v. 17); "If you continue in my word, you are truly my disciples; and you will know the truth, and the truth will make you free" (8:31); "I am the way, and the truth, and the life" (14:6). The truth of the gospel is not a concept, a proposition, or a theorem. The truth is a person, Jesus Christ.

John Calvin began his *Institutes of the Christian Religion* by stating, "Nearly all the wisdom we possess, that is to say, true and sound wisdom, consists of two parts: the knowledge of God and of ourselves."[2] The consistent witness of Scripture is that Jesus Christ

2. John Calvin, *Institutes of the Christian Religion,* trans. Ford Lewis Battles, ed. John T. McNeill, Library of Christian Classics (Philadelphia: The Westminster Press, 1960), 1.1.1. (35).

is the truth about who God is, the truth about who we are, and the truth about who we are meant to be. "No one has ever seen God," proclaims the apostle, "the only Son, who is in the bosom of the Father, he has made him known" (John 1:18, RSV). In Christ, God is revealed as God truly is, not as we might imagine God to be, or hope or fear that God is. "God" means many different things to people; apart from God's self-disclosure, we are left to the imagination of our hearts. But we do not have to imagine, for God has made himself known in a way we can understand: in the incarnation, life, death, resurrection, and ascension of Jesus Christ.

The consistent witness of Scripture is that Jesus Christ is the truth about who God is, the truth about who we are, and the truth about who we are meant to be.

In Christ we not only know who God is, we also know who we are and who we are meant to be. Self-knowledge is shaded by self-idealizations and self-projections, but through Christ we can see ourselves honestly, and in Christ we can know who we were created to be. In the words of the Nicene Creed, Jesus Christ is "God from God, Light from Light, true God from true God," who "for us and for our salvation . . . became truly human."[3] Jesus Christ, God in person, is the answer to Pilate's question and to ours. The fourth great end calls us to preserve the truth that Christ is the Truth.

You Shall Have No Other Gods Before Me

The first human obligation in response to God's covenantal love is to have no gods but the LORD God. The second requirement follows: "You shall not make for yourself an idol . . . You shall not bow down to them or worship them" (Exodus 20:4–5). Thus, the third great purpose of the church is not to maintain worship that is "simply divine" (or "reliably traditional" or "inventively contemporary") but to uphold the worship of *God*. "Maintenance of divine worship" is paired with "preservation of the truth" because without the truth about God we will end up worshiping the gods of our desiring.

Orthodoxy is sometimes associated with rigid adherence to theological dogma, but it is helpful to know that orthodoxy (*orthōs doxa* = right belief) is intimately connected to worship (*orthōs doxadzō* = right praise). Orthodoxy's primary significance

3. Presbyterian Church (U.S.A.), *Book of Confessions: Study Edition* (Louisville, KY: Geneva Press, 1999), 1.2.

is found in its lived truth within worshiping congregations. In an institutionalized, market-driven, entrepreneurial culture, worship of the only God—Father, Son, and Holy Spirit—is in constant danger of being engulfed in a sea of functional unitarianism, pop therapy, and institutional self-promotion. The danger is not confined to megachurches, liberal churches, or careless churches. In a fragmented ecclesial landscape of competing denominations and congregations, the temptation is ever-present to stir into the liturgical mix a little—or more than a little—self-help, entertainment, group building, and organizational promotion.

The Reformed tradition has always been aware that worship can drift away from God toward preoccupation with ourselves. Gratitude for God's grace can be displaced by what we imagine worship can do to fulfill us. Calls to worship, hymns, prayers, and sermons may become words about us rather than proclamation of the triune God who creates and sustains all things, who reconciles the world to himself, and who leads us into truth and faithfulness.

The Reformed tradition has always been aware that worship can drift away from God toward preoccupation with ourselves. Gratitude for God's grace can be displaced by what we imagine worship can do to fulfill us.

Because Jesus Christ is the Truth about God and ourselves, witness to the Truth must be at the heart of worship, forming and enlivening every element of the service. Scripture read and interpreted faithfully, together with sacraments celebrated in testimony to the gospel, is essential if we are to maintain the worship of God. The significance of faithful worship is not confined to worship services themselves, for maintenance of the worship of God is necessary to maintain the congregation in faithful mission and ministry.

Word and sacrament are the guarantors of divine worship, yet oral reading of Scripture often is inconsistent, flat, disinterested, and virtually impossible to listen to. Too many sermons are more about the preacher or the congregation than the gospel. Baptism is regularly minimized by momentary focus on a baby rather than on union with Christ in death and new life. The Lord's Supper is often an exercise in silent introspection instead of communion with the risen, living Lord of life. When these real and present dangers threaten Word and sacrament, all of worship is at risk. Then, inevitably, worship becomes a pastime designed to please us, not our grateful response to the God who continues to give himself to us.

Praying and Believing

Presbyterians are not fluent in church Latin, but one ancient church motto is worth remembering: *lex orandi, lex credendi* = rule of praying, rule of believing. The motto is generally taken to mean the worship of the church shapes the faith of the church. It is a shorthand way of saying how we worship molds what worshipers believe. Who doubts it? The hymns we sing (and those we avoid), the sacraments we celebrate (or neglect), the sermons we listen to (or ignore), what we pray for (and what we ignore in prayer), the vestments ministers wear (or shun), and the ways we participate (or remain passive) all influence the contours of belief within the con¬gregation. One of the reasons for making preservation of divine worship one of the church's central purposes is the recognition that the faith of the church is formed by the worship of the church.

Worship that has Christ as its matter and substance . . .

> forms a church that believes Christ and through him believes in one God, Father, Son, and Holy Spirit;
> trusts Christ and through him trusts the promises of God and the power of the Holy Spirit;
> is loyal to Christ and through him is unwavering in love of God and life in the Spirit.

On the other hand, worship that has as its matter and substance human wants and needs, aspirations and causes, forms a church that believes in itself, trusts its programs, and is loyal to its institutions.

The worship of the assembly is so central to the preservation of the truth that the Latin saying can be reversed: the church's belief shapes its worship. Deciding how a congregation worships should involve more than matters of custom, taste, hospitality, and preference. Pastors, elders, musicians, and other worship planners must pay the closest theological attention to the order of worship and all worship's elements to ensure that Word and sacrament are at the heart of worship, and that all else flows from Word and sacrament. The purpose of theologically shaped worship is not liturgical fussiness, or even liturgical renewal, but rather "setting forth Christ to us, and in him the treasures of heavenly grace."[4] Human needs and aspirations are not irrelevant, of course, yet the gospel frees them from willful craving and consumption, so they can

4. Calvin, *Institutes,* 4.14.17 (1292).

find their true fulfillment through Christ's grace, God's love, and the communion of the Holy Spirit.

Although preservation of the truth and maintenance of divine worship are inextricably linked, neither is swallowed up in the other. Congregational attention to the truth of the gospel animates education, nurtures disciples, focuses mission, builds budgets, guides service, and envisions new possibilities. Congregational attention to the worship of God deepens daily prayer, directs spiritual disciplines, alters vocational integrity, clarifies the leading of the Holy Spirit, empowers mission, and enables sacrificial service. Truth and worship form a Möbius strip of continuous interaction in the life of the church.

Truth and worship form a Möbius strip of continuous interaction in the life of the church.

Spiritual Practice

Travel through the worship bulletin of a recent Sunday worship service, praying the prayers, humming the hymn tunes while reading the hymn texts, reading the Scripture texts aloud, and "seeing" the sacraments through closed eyes. What is Christ saying to you and to your congregation? Where is the Spirit leading?

Questions for Reflection

What elements in the worship of the congregation direct us to God, and what elements are about us? What is the ratio?

Is it arrogant to talk about *the* truth in religion?

If divine worship helps preserve the truth, how important is it that the truth of the gospel shape congregational worship?

Session 4

The Church and the World

Scripture

John 17:15–18 Because we are not of the world, we are sent into the world.

Prayer

Gracious God: you called us to be the church of Jesus Christ. Keep us one in faith and service, breaking bread together, and telling good news to the world. Lord of all: order the unruly powers, deal with injustice, feed and satisfy the longing peoples, so that in freedom your children may enjoy the world you made; Through Jesus Christ our Lord. Amen.[1]

Introduction

Moving outward from the church's core purposes of preserving the truth and maintaining divine worship, we encounter the paired great ends "shelter, nurture, and spiritual fellowship of the children of God" and "promotion of social righteousness." At first glance, they may seem like an odd couple; on closer examination, we can see them as a dynamic expression of the relationship between the inner life of the church and its outward life in society. As the *ekklēsia,* a people called away from "the way things are" into God's new Way, we live within the communion of the Holy Spirit, we are defended against damaging aspects of the culture, and we grow in faith and faithfulness. As the *ekklēsia,* a people called by Christ, we are sent into the world to foster God's Way in the midst of the way things are. Churches are called to be different from the world, but not to withdraw from the world; churches are called to serve boldly in the world, but not to neglect spiritual nurture within the community of faith.

"Shelter, nurture, and spiritual fellowship of the children of God" characterizes the quality of new life we are called to live within the

1. *The Worshipbook* (Philadelphia: The Westminster Press, 1970), 31. Used with permission.

church. "Promotion of social righteousness" characterizes the way we are called to live in society. They are not juxtaposed as unrelated purposes of the church, much less as contradictory purposes that require us to prefer one to the other. One has to do with the church's inner life of fostering mature discipleship. These ministries of the church equip men and women to live God's Way in the world. The other has to do with the church's outer life of bold discipleship in work, school, family, and public life. This mission of the church leads to renewed reliance on the grace of Christ, the love of God, and the community of the Spirit.

The practical relationship between the two is not self-evident, however. Within both congregations and denominations, the two purposes are in tension as often as in harmony. The church is called to recover the essential interaction between its inner and outer life.

Maturity

Shelter, nurture, and spiritual fellowship draw our attention to some of the most appealing aspects of congregational life. They suggest relationships more than programs, personal connections instead of organizational structure, and fulfillment rather than obligation. The second great end does not present shelter, nurture, and spiritual fellowship as descriptions of actual church life, however, but as intentions that congregations and denominations should pursue. We know they are sometimes fulfilled but often unsatisfied. Yet, whether realized or not, they should never be sentimentalized, as if the church's goal was simply to provide a comfortable, nurturing environment for Christians.

The first step toward understanding this great purpose of church life is to realize that "of the children of God" modifies each of the elements in this somewhat awkward trio, not simply the final one: shelter *of the children of God,* nurture *of the children of God,* and spiritual fellowship *of the children of God.* This great purpose of the church's life is concerned with naming *whose* we are as well as how we are to live.

Children of God is not merely religious language for "all people" or a routine synonym for *Christians.* We are not natural children of God. The New Testament identifies us as *adopted* children, welcomed into God's household by an act of gracious love. "But when the fullness of time had come," says Paul, "God sent his Son, born of a woman, born under the law . . . so that we might receive adoption as children. And because you are children, God has sent the Spirit of his Son into our hearts, crying, 'Abba! Father!' " (Galatians 4:4–6). We are not children of God by birthright; each of us is Christ's adopted sister or brother, and thus we are brothers and sisters to one another.

As adopted children in God's household, we are no longer bound to what Paul calls "the elemental spirits of the world" (Galatians 4:3)—what we might call the "spirit of the times" or "the way things are in the world." The church is called to be a shelter from corrosive elements in our culture that turn us away from God, from one another, and from people who remain in captivity to harmful social realities. The church is not an escape from reality, however; it is called to be a Spirit-shaped community where we are nurtured to maturity in Christ. Eugene Peterson's paraphrase of Ephesians 4:14–15 puts this well: "No prolonged infancies among us, please. We'll not tolerate babes in the woods, small children who are an easy mark for imposters. God wants us to grow up, to know the whole truth and tell it in love—like Christ in everything."[2]

The church is called to be more than a successful full-service provider of religious goods and services. The church purposes to be the household of God that nurtures us to maturity in Christ, forming us as a community of the Spirit that lives faithfully in the world.

The church is called to be more than a successful full-service provider of religious goods and services. The church purposes to be the household of God that nurtures us to maturity in Christ, forming us as a community of the Spirit that lives faithfully in the world.

Let Justice Roll Down

Amos 5:24—"Let justice [Hebrew *mishpat*] roll down like waters, and righteousness [*tsedaqa*] like an ever-flowing stream"—is one of the best-known verses in the Old Testament. A familiar verse in the New Testament is Matthew 5:6, "Blessed are those who hunger and thirst for righteousness [Gr. *dikaiosunē*], for they will be filled." In Hebrew, *justice* and *righteousness* are synonyms that describe both God and the qualities of a social order lived under God's rule. In Greek, *justice* and *righteousness* are so closely related that one

2. Scripture taken from THE MESSAGE. Copyright © 1993, 1994, 1995, 1996, 2000, 2001, 2002. Used by permission of NavPress Publishing Group.

word—*dikaiosunē*—signifies both and can be translated into English as either.

Common English usage generally employs *righteousness* to describe personal qualities and *justice* to describe characteristics of the social and political order. This may be too sharp a distinction, however, for the two English words describe aspects of one biblical reality. Even in English, one can be properly substituted for the other. Second Corinthians 9:9 could be translated as "As it is written, 'He scatters abroad, he gives to the poor; his *justice* endures forever.'" Romans 3:5 could be rendered as "But if our *unrighteousness* serves to confirm the *righteousness* of God . . ." The fourth beatitude could be translated properly as "Blessed are those who hunger and thirst for *justice*" (Matthew 5:6).

Promotion of social righteousness is the church's action for justice in social structures and righteousness in personal and group life. The meaning of justice, and especially social justice, is not self-evident, however. The American political and judicial system equates justice with the attainment of personal and group rights. Because one assertion of rights is likely to conflict with another assertion of rights, justice is often reduced to the adjudication of adversarial disputes between rival claims. Rights-based justice appeals to *fairness* as the standard for determining a just outcome, but since fairness is in the eyes of opposing plaintiffs, justice must rely on legislative or judicial procedures. When justice is restricted to rights, the promotion of social justice can become a zero-sum game.

Alasdair MacIntyre draws attention to "the intimidating range of questions about what justice requires and permits, to which alternative and incompatible answers are offered by contending individuals and groups within contemporary societies."[3] The church has a distinct perspective to bring to disputes about social issues, one that does not simply echo clashing voices. Scripture and Christian tradition have much to say about justice. The church's responsibility to do justice and to seek justice is clear. However, Scripture and Christian tradition do not reduce God's justice to fairness. They do not assume justice is established through the conflict between competing rights. In Scripture, justice/righteousness has more to do with obligations than with rights, with relationships than with clashes, with covenants than with laws, with peace than with

3. Alasdair MacIntyre, *Whose Justice? Which Rationality?* (Notre Dame, IN: University of Notre Dame Press, 1988), 1.

verdicts, and with communion than with adversarial conflict. In its essential calling to promote social justice, the church has something unique to contribute to "liberty and justice for *all.*"

In Scripture, justice/righteousness has more to do with obligations than with rights, with relationships than with clashes, with covenants than with laws, with peace than with verdicts, and with communion than with adversarial conflict. In its essential calling to promote social justice, the church has something unique to contribute to "liberty and justice for all."

The Church Inside Out

The biblical formulation for the relationship between the Christian community and the culture is embedded in Christian consciousness: we are to be in the world, but not of it. Paul implores Christians: "Conform no longer to the pattern of this present world, but be transformed by the renewal of your minds" (Romans 12:2, Revised English Bible). He also counsels against separatism from "people in general who are immoral or extortioners or swindlers or idolaters; to avoid them you would have to withdraw from society altogether" (1 Corinthians 5:10, Revised English Bible). *In,* but not of—no flight from the realities of the world in which we live; no conformity to the way things are. This is not a simple matter. How do we engage the world without becoming captive to it?

Jürgen Moltmann speaks of the church's double crisis *of relevance* and *of identity.* "The more theology and the church attempt to become relevant to the problems of the present day, the more deeply they are drawn into the crisis of their own Christian identity. The more they attempt to assert their identity in traditional dogmas, rights, and moral notions, the more unbelievable and irrelevant they become. This double crisis is more accurately described as the *identity-involvement dilemma.*"[4] Pairing the inner and outer life of the church in a unified understanding of its place in the world helps overcome Moltmann's double crisis. Shelter, nurture, and spiritual fellowship on the one hand, promotion of social righteousness on the other, means no Christian identity without involvement in society,

4. Jürgen Moltmann, *The Crucified God,* trans. R. A. Wilson and John Bowden (New York: Harper & Row, 1973), 7.

no engagement in the pursuit of justice without the maturity of the children of God.

Shelter, nurture, and spiritual fellowship on the one hand, promotion of social righteousness on the other, means no Christian identity without involvement in society, no engagement in the pursuit of justice without the maturity of the children of God.

John Calvin called the church our mother: "For there is no other way to enter into life unless this mother conceive us in her womb, give us birth, nourish us at her breast, and lastly, unless she keep us under her care and guidance." The people of God are gathered into the church "not only that they may be nourished by her help and ministry as long as they are infants and children, but also that they may be guided by her motherly care until they mature and at last reach the goal of faith."[5]

This lovely description of the shelter, nurture, and spiritual fellowship of the children of God does not suggest an enclosed sanctuary, separated from the concerns of the world. The church's care and guidance led the churches of Geneva into efforts to improve society. Calvin established the diaconate to lead the church in care for the poor, refugees, widows and orphans, and others in need. The church worked to provide educational opportunities and medical care, lobbied for a sanitary sewer system, and even searched Europe for a more economical cooking stove for poor people. Reform of the church's inner life led naturally to reform of society. Spiritually mature churches work for righteousness in their societies.

5. John Calvin, *Institutes of the Christian Religion*, trans. Ford Lewis Battles, ed. John T. McNeill, Library of Christian Classics (Philadelphia: The Westminster Press, 1960), 4.1.4 (1016), 4.1.1 (1012).

Spiritual Practice

The church in Calvin's Geneva was active in refugee relief; today's world is marked by too many refugees in too many places. Pray each day in the coming week for a specific country where refugees need the shelter, nurture, and spiritual fellowship of the children of God.

Questions for Reflection

How has the nurture provided by your congregation made you a more mature disciple of Jesus Christ in the last year?

Does promotion of social righteousness lead to the church's involvement in partisan politics?

Is there a danger that the church's shelter, nurture, and fellowship can become conformed to the pattern of this present world?

Faithful Witness

Scripture

Romans 10:9–17 How are people to know Christ unless they hear the gospel?

Prayer

God of love, who sent Jesus Christ to seek and save the lost: may we who have been found by him value those who do not believe, and never shun neighbors who reject you. Remembering how our faith was given, may we preach good news with goodwill, trusting you to follow up your word, so that people may hear and believe and come to you; through Jesus Christ our Lord. Amen.[1]

Introduction

The first and last great purposes of the church's life form a natural pair. "Proclamation of the gospel for the salvation of humankind" and "exhibition of the Kingdom of Heaven to the world" direct us to the substance and shape of the church's witness. Proclaiming the good news of salvation in Jesus Christ tells the world what it does not know. Exhibiting the shape of new life in Christ displays to the world an unfamiliar way of living. Together, they invite people to faith in the One who is their Savior and Lord.

The minute we move beyond general affirmations, however, we encounter confusion and even disagreement about every element in the formulations. What, exactly, is the *gospel?* Is it the whole of the Bible, can it be summarized in the Apostles' Creed, or is it a simple formula? What makes it *news* anyone should care about? Is it *good* for everyone? Even if we are sure what it is, how are we supposed to *proclaim* it? What in the world does it mean to be *saved?* Are we saved from something, for something, or both? Is this gospel really meant for all of humankind? Is salvation denied to people who are not Christians? What is this "Kingdom of Heaven" we are supposed

1. *The Worshipbook* (Philadelphia: The Westminster Press, 1970), 188, alt. Used with permission.

to *exhibit?* Does the world pay any attention to what the church says and does?

Our problems with the pairing of proclamation and exhibition may be magnified by the realization that they call each one of us to personal action. These two great ends have pointed implications for our personal lives in work, school, neighborhood, and home. What do we have to say to colleagues and friends about our faith in Christ? Does our manner of life bear noticeable marks of discipleship in Christ? Our problems with these two great purposes go beyond definition, challenging our customary silence and our easy accommodation to the way things are in our culture.

Proclamation

The English word *gospel,* or *good news,* renders the Greek *euangelion,* which also gives us the English *evangelism*. Presbyterians are notoriously uneasy about evangelism that actually proclaims the gospel to people outside the church, equating it with stadium crusades and televangelists. An old joke:

> What is the Presbyterian evangelism strategy?
> *Unlocking the church doors on Sunday morning.*

Hesitance to proclaim the gospel has something to do with uncertainty about just what the gospel is. Insecurity about the shape of the gospel may result from ambiguity about what salvation is and about who will be saved.

As with most things about Christian faith, it helps to turn attention away from our hesitance, uncertainty, insecurity, and ambiguity, and look instead at what God has done and is doing in the world. From Genesis to Revelation, Scripture witnesses to the gracious presence in human life of the one God, creator and redeemer of all that is. Scripture also gives doleful testimony to the sin and suffering of humankind, from Cain's murder of Abel to the deadly beast of Revelation. From beginning to end, the astonishing news is that God is constantly faithful to us: "if we are faithless, he remains faithful—for he cannot deny himself" (2 Timothy 2:13).

The good news tells us God's faithfulness to us is lived out in the incarnation, life, teaching, crucifixion, resurrection, and ascension of Jesus Christ, who is Emmanuel, God with us. "No one has ever seen God," says John's Gospel. Yet God is not a remote, unknowable mystery: "God the only Son, who is at the Father's side, has made

God known" (John 1:18, Common English Bible). Our knowledge of God comes directly from God, not from ourselves. Human speculation cannot arrive at true knowledge of God because our hopes and fears, our needs and our apathy, will always result in an idol, a god of our own imagining. Thankfully, we do not have to make guesses about God because God has revealed himself to us in terms we can understand—in human terms, in a human life.

God has united himself to us in Jesus Christ so that, in union with Christ, we are reunited with God. "And this is eternal life," says John, "that they may know you, the only true God, and Jesus Christ whom you have sent" (John 17:3). What is "eternal life"? It is not simply an unending extension of time any more than depth is an extension of height and width. Eternal life is life in a new dimension. It commences with our faith that "the Word became flesh and dwelt among us, full of grace and truth"—dwelt among us in life and in death and in resurrection—and that "we have beheld his glory, glory as of the only Son from the Father" (John 1:14, RSV). Life in Christ is the new dimension of loving God—and loving other people—with heart, soul, mind, and strength.

God has united himself to us in Jesus Christ so that, in union with Christ, we are reunited with God.

God's New Way in the World

Robin Lane Fox's detailed study *Pagans and Christians* explores the causes behind Christianity's centuries-long expansion throughout the pagan world. The reasons are multiple and complex, but the most significant factor seems to be that Christianity offered "an alternative community and range of values to those who were disenchanted by the display of riches, by the harshness of the exercise of power and the progressive hardening of the gradations of rank and degree" in the Greco-Roman world.[2]

The evidence shows people were initially drawn to Christian faith because they saw Christian communities that encompassed all social classes, that included women as well as men and poor as well as rich in leadership, and that were conspicuously generous in sharing resources with people in need, outside of the Christian community as well as within it. Furthermore, they saw Christians who were willing to die for their faith as *martyrs* (that is, *witnesses*), exhibiting a depth of conviction unknown among the pagan religions.

2. Robin Lane Fox, *Pagans and Christians* (San Francisco: Harper & Row, 1986), 321.

In short, Christians of the first four centuries exhibited the kingdom of heaven to the world. Kingdom of *heaven* (the Gospel of Matthew's term for kingdom of *God*) sounds oddly archaic to contemporary American ears. "The Way of God" or "God's new Way in the world" is a paraphrase that may shed light on the kingdom of God. The rewording is not an arbitrary invention, for the Gospels echo the Old Testament expression "Way of the Lord," and Acts relates that the earliest Christians were called "the Way."[3] The Way of God suggests both a difference from "the way things are" and the new direction that Christians are called to follow.

The church exhibits the kingdom of heaven to the world when it displays a character and quality of life noticeably different from the surrounding culture. It also shows God's new Way as Christians demonstrate a distinctive character and quality of life in family, neighborhood, school, work, and civic life. None of this comes naturally or easily, however. That is why the early church required one to three years of preparation for baptism, focusing as sharply on how Christians lived as on what Christians believed. Jesus' definitive proclamation—"The time is fulfilled, and the kingdom of God is at hand; repent, and believe in the gospel" (Mark 1:15, RSV)—remains his call to the church: *God's time is flowing into this time, and God's new Way in the world is touching the way things are; turn around, walk in the path of God's Way. Believe that this news is good, trust it, and remain steadfast in it.*

> *The church exhibits the kingdom of heaven to the world when it displays a character and quality of life noticeably different from the surrounding culture.*

What does the world see when it looks at the church? If what it sees is simply a religious organization that shapes its life by familiar social conventions, the world will have little reason to keep looking at the church, scant cause to wonder what prompts its behavior, and no incentive to inquire about its faith.

Show and Tell

Fox's wide-ranging study of Christianity's expansion does not claim the alternative character of Christian community, by itself, produced converts. While sweeping social diversity and conspicuous charity were enduring marks of early Christian communities, there was more to it. The leveling of social, gender, class, and rank divisions grew

3. See Acts 9:2; 19:9, 23; 22:4; 24:14, 22.

from a distinctive ideal of human equality: "in Christ, taught the Christians, all were equal and the distinctions of rank and degree were irrelevant."[4] *In Christ* taught the Christians, for God's gracious presence in the world broke down dividing walls. It was through baptism in union with Christ that "there is no longer Jew or Greek, there is no longer slave or free, there is no longer male and female; for all of you are one in Christ Jesus" (Galatians 3:28). All one *in Christ Jesus*.

In Christ, through Christ, with Christ, the church exhibited God's Way to the world. When some in the world took notice, the church was prepared to proclaim the gospel of the grace of Christ, the love of God, and the communion of the Holy Spirit, the good news that converted women and men to new life. Proclamation of salvation grew from exhibition of salvation in the life of the Christian community and the lives of Christian people. Proclamation without exhibition always rings hollow; exhibition without proclamation always appears arbitrary.

Proclamation of salvation grew from exhibition of salvation in the life of the Christian community and the lives of Christian people. Proclamation without exhibition always rings hollow; exhibition without proclamation always appears arbitrary.

Fox's inquiry into the life of the early Christian communities is relevant to contemporary Christian existence because our situation is more like the church's first centuries than the long centuries of Christendom that followed. Christendom is now a fading memory; no longer can we assume a "Christian culture" in which the church's faith and values are assumed. Christianity in Europe and North America may not yet be as small a minority as in the first four centuries, but it faces similar realities. The church cannot live as if its gospel is widely known, understood, and valued, let alone believed. The church cannot imagine it is accorded social leadership in compassion, peace, and justice. The church cannot assume its life informs and shapes American culture, but it must now be alert to the ways American culture shapes the church.

The first and the last of the church's great ends point us in the same direction. Our purpose is to declare the good news of God's Way in how we live and in what we have to say. Presbyterian talk

4. Fox, 336.

about mission these days usually focuses on activities, programs, and budgets. Our primary missional challenge, however, is more about who we are and what we have to say than it is about multiplying initiatives and increasing mission dollars. The character of the church's life together will shape both its social witness and its public proclamation of the gospel. Perhaps more importantly, the character of the church's life together will shape the private and public life of each Christian, and will give each Christian a faith worth talking about.

Spiritual Practice

The great ends of the church are not limited to one denomination or nation. Follow the cycle of the *Book of Common Worship*'s daily prayer by praying on successive mornings for the witness of the church in Europe, in Africa, in Asia, in the Middle East, in the Pacific region, and in North America; and on successive evenings for the Roman Catholic Church, Orthodox and Coptic churches, Episcopal and Methodist churches, Baptist and other free churches, Pentecostal churches, and Reformed, Presbyterian, and Lutheran churches.

Questions for Reflection

How would friends say you best witness to Christ—in your words or in your actions?

What does the world see when it looks at your congregation?

What are ways for individuals to witness to Christ in daily life?

Put These Things into Practice

Scripture

1 Timothy 4:11–16 Be doers of what you have learned, not merely talkers about ideas.

Prayer

Almighty God: you poured out the Holy Spirit on believers at Pentecost, drawing them together in the mission of the church. Give us great enthusiasm for your work, and keep your Spirit with us, so that, united and in peace with one another, we may live new lives as ambassadors of Jesus Christ, who is head of the church, our Savior and our strength. Amen.[1]

Introduction

A perennial problem in church education is the temptation to learn *about* something rather than exploring more fully the truth of who God is and who we are. Too often, study in the church keeps God at a safe distance. Bible study can become an exercise in historical archaeology, unearthing what people used to believe long ago and far away. Theological study can become abstract examination of "theories" of the atonement and other central Christian affirmations. Ethical study can become our self-assured discussion of what others should do. Adult studies can easily avoid honest examination of congregational life and the lives of class participants. The result of all this is an unspoken suspicion that God is distant, inactive in life here and now, essentially irrelevant Monday through Saturday.

The great ends of the church is not simply an artifact from the early twentieth century, a study topic, or an appreciated formula. These six great ends, preserved for more than a century, remain enduring purposes for the lives of congregations, presbyteries, and General Assembly agencies. They provide a way of analyzing the church's faith and life honestly. They also set out the fundamental

1. *The Worshipbook* (Philadelphia: The Westminster Press, 1970), 199. Used with permission.

commitments for which the church exists and toward which it should strive.

Our task in this concluding session is to imagine ways the church—especially this congregation—can move toward a deeper, more comprehensive fulfillment of its reason for being. Another task before us is to see ourselves, active participants in God's purposes, sharing life together in the congregation, the presbytery, and the denomination. Our ultimate task is to persevere in working toward each of the great ends rather than abandoning them as we move on to another topic.

The Letter of James captures the danger of study in haunting words: "You must be doers of the word and not only hearers who mislead themselves. Those who hear but don't do the word are like those who look at their faces in a mirror. They look at themselves, walk away, and immediately forget what they were like" (James 1:22–24, Common English Bible).

Lex Orandi, Lex Credendi

Pastors quickly learn few things are more hazardous to their ministry than making precipitous changes in worship. Congregational worship is the time in the life of the church when the largest number of members gather. Study groups, mission projects, fellowship events, and all other church activities are for the few. For many church members, worship *is* church. Therefore, it is understandable any change in worship will please some while upsetting others. Debates over changes in congregational worship invariably revolve around meeting the needs and preferences of the largest number of members possible while minimizing the discontent of others.

When the shape of worship depends on the preference of worshipers, it becomes more about us than about God in Christ reconciling the world to himself and entrusting to us the message of reconciliation (2 Corinthians 5:19). What happens in worship forms (or malforms) the fundamental faith and life of the church, and so the truth of the gospel and the discipleship of the church are at stake in every congregation every Lord's Day. Perhaps that is why the middle two great ends are couched in defensive terms. The other fundamental purposes use bold language—proclaim, nurture, promote, exhibit—while the central two warn us to *maintain* divine worship and *preserve* the truth. Truth and worship seem to be endangered.

Ordering worship apart from deep knowledge of the gospel's truth is always in danger of becoming just one more activity that is religious. Insisting on theological precision apart from praise of God is always in danger of becoming just one more ideology that is religious. It doesn't end there. Religious activity and ideology . . .

- endanger the proclamation of the gospel by twisting it into institutional marketing;
- endanger the shelter, nurture, and spiritual fellowship of the children of God by reducing them to religious goods and services;
- endanger promotion of social righteousness by hardening it into partisan politics;
- endanger the exhibition of the kingdom of heaven by degrading it into ecclesial self-promotion.

The tasks of maintenance and preservation are the essential underpinning of the church's great purposes.

There is no one right way to assess congregational commitment to maintaining the worship of God and preserving the truth of the gospel. Every pastor, every session, and every member is called to ask: "What does worship in our congregation communicate to members and visitors about the shape of Christian faith?" "How do the central affirmations of Christian faith shape worship in our congregation?" Two key documents and their interaction may help answer the questions. The Nicene Creed—the foundational articulation of Christian belief—narrates the shape of the gospel and establishes the basic vocabulary, grammar, and syntax of Christian faith. The *Book of Order*'s Directory for Worship sets out broad principles for faithful worship. Serious, sustained attention to each of these and to their interaction will provide guidance for congregational maintenance of divine worship and preservation of the truth.

There is no one right way to assess congregational commitment to maintaining the worship of God and preserving the truth of the gospel.

Just Church

Some observers of contemporary church life categorize congregations as "chaplaincies" and "missional churches." Chaplaincy churches focus on the internal life of the congregation, shaping programs and activities that serve the church's members. Missional churches focus on outreach to those beyond the walls of the congregation and the boundaries of the denomination. The categories are far too broad, of course. No church is exclusively one or the other. Virtually every congregation is properly concerned with the well-being of the church and its members. Virtually every congregation is properly concerned with the well-being of people and groups beyond the church.

The rough categories serve a purpose, however. The question is not whether a congregation is exclusively one or the other, but whether a congregation sustains a proper relationship between the two. Upholding the balance between "shelter, nurture, and spiritual fellowship of the children of God" and "promotion of social righteousness" is a spiritual issue, not merely a managerial, "best practices" matter. It is a spiritual issue because fidelity to the gospel requires both, and because concentration on one at the expense of the other distorts both.

Upholding the balance between "shelter, nurture, and spiritual fellowship of the children of God" and "promotion of social righteousness" . . . is a spiritual issue because fidelity to the gospel requires both, and because concentration on one at the expense of the other distorts both.

Paul's prayers for Christian congregations demonstrate the biblical centrality of building up the body of Christ.[2] Jesus' announcement of his divine mission is the pattern for the church's mission to all who are poor now, hungry now, and disconsolate now.[3] Scripture does not divide faithfulness into alternatives—ecclesial nurture *or* communal righteousness, spiritual fellowship *or* social justice. Nurture and justice are two sides of the same discipleship coin. Scripture warns against attention to the shared inner life of the people of God at the expense of justice in society.[4] Scripture also warns against imagining we can fulfill God's will in society while neglecting the grace of

2. Romans 1:8–10; 1 Corinthians 1:4–9; Ephesians 1:16–19; Philippians 1:3–11; Colossians 1:3–14; 1 Thessalonians 1:2–3; 2 Thessalonians 1:3–4.
3. Luke 4:16–21; 7:18–24. See Jesus' "Sermon on the Plain," Luke 6:20–26.
4. See Isaiah 58:1–7.

Christ, the love of God, and the communion of the Holy Spirit.[5]

The relationship between the church for itself and the church for others is easy to assess. Jesus said, "Where your treasure is, there your heart will be also" (Matthew 6:21). The church budget is a reliable guide to congregational commitments (just as our checkbooks are a reliable guide to our personal priorities). Money is only part of the story, however, for a survey of church newsletters will reveal the relationship between programs and activities for church members and those for people and organizations who suffer poverty, hunger, homelessness, racism, and other forms of social injustice.

A distinction is sometimes made between "compassion" and "justice," equating compassion with short-term services and justice with systemic solutions. The dichotomy is false if it leads to preferring one or the other. Social righteousness requires *both* immediate action to alleviate deprivation and suffering *and* long-term action to rectify societal, political, and legal inequities. Throughout, the promotion of social righteousness requires congregational nurture, and congregational nurture leads to the promotion of social righteousness.

Why Christian?

The Presbyterian *Book of Order* used to contain the declaration "the church is the provisional demonstration of what God intends for humanity." I once heard that statement in a sermon; my immediate reaction was "I hope not." The church is an ambiguous blend of faithfulness and faithlessness, and so what it "demonstrates" always falls short of God's intention for the church itself, let alone for all humankind. Yet the imperfect church is called to exhibit the kingdom of God to the world, to be a provisional demonstration that God's Way is the way for all.

Yet the imperfect church is called to exhibit the kingdom of God to the world, to be a provisional demonstration that God's Way is the way for all.

5. See Romans 2:1–24.

Congregations engage in periodic self-studies. As valuable as these may be, they rarely take sufficient account of how the congregation is perceived by people who are not part of the congregation or people who are not part of any church at all. If the church is on display, what does the world see? When the church speaks, what does the world hear? If news coverage is an accurate indication, the church is known by its scandals. If movies and television reflect the world's views, churches are considered ineffectual or distasteful. If best-sellers are an accurate barometer, the church is judged to be deluded or dangerous or both. While congregations may enjoy a somewhat better reputation than denominations, they are regularly accused of hypocrisy and being self-serving.

The church's negative image in news coverage, movies, and books may conceal a more common response to the church: indifference. Churches appear to be little different from other social institutions, a reflection of society's racial, economic, and class segmentation. It may appear the church has done the unimaginable, inverting Jesus' saying by being of the world, but not in it.[6] Congregations and denominations should assess honestly whether their lives display God's Way in the world, a Way the world might find intriguing, attractive, and captivating. Congregations and denominations should also assess what people overhear when they listen to what we say.

The church's calling to proclaim the gospel and exhibit God's new Way in the world is not confined to the congregation as an organization. It is also, perhaps even primarily, the calling of individual Christians. Our lives—observed Monday through Saturday by our neighbors, fellow students, and co-workers—say more about Christian faith and life, and say it more persuasively, than Sunday church programs and pronouncements. If what others see in us is no different from what they see in themselves, it will never occur to them to ask about the faith that shapes us. If what they see makes them curious, we must be able to proclaim the gospel, giving an account of the hope that is in us (1 Peter 3:15).

6. Donald C. Posterski, *Reinventing Evangelism: New Strategies for Presenting Christ in Today's World* (Downers Grove, IL: InterVarsity Press, 1989), 28. See also George R. Hunsberger and Craig Van Gelder, *The Church between Gospel and Culture* (Grand Rapids, MI: Eerdmans Publishing, 1996), 292–297.

Spiritual Practice

Keep a journal for the next two months, jotting down thoughts about your congregation's life as if you were an outside observer. Also, write the names of people you encounter, reflecting on what of the gospel they see in you.

Questions for Reflection

What is the relationship between the truth of the gospel and diversity of beliefs?

How can church commitment to social justice avoid partisan politics?

How comfortable are you in talking about your faith in Christ? What steps will you take to gain comfort and experience in talking about Christ?

Suggestions for Further Study

Alston, Wallace M., Jr. *The Church of the Living God: A Reformed Perspective*. Louisville: Westminster John Knox Press, 2002.

Byars, Ronald P. *Christian Worship: Glorifying and Enjoying God*. Louisville: Geneva Press, 2000.

Dean, Kenda Creasy. *Almost Christian: What the Faith of Our Teenagers Is Telling the American Church*. New York: Oxford University Press, 2010.

Guder, Darrell L. *The Continuing Conversion of the Church*. Grand Rapids, MI: Eerdmans, 2000.

Peterson, Eugene. *Practice Resurrection: A Conversation on Growing Up in Christ*. Grand Rapids, MI: Eerdmans, 2010.

Plantinga, Cornelius, Jr., and Sue A. Rozeboom, *Discerning the Spirits: A Guide to Thinking about Christian Worship Today*. Grand Rapids, MI: Eerdmans, 2003.

Rigby, Cynthia L. *Promotion of Social Righteousness*. Louisville: Witherspoon Press, 2010.

Russell, Letty M. *Church in the Round: Feminist Interpretation of the Church*. Louisville: Westminster John Knox Press, 1993.

Small, Joseph D. *To Be Reformed: Living the Tradition*. Louisville: Witherspoon Press, 2010.

Small, Joseph D. *Preservation of the Truth*. Louisville: Witherspoon Press, 2005.

CPSIA information can be obtained at www.ICGtesting.com
Printed in the USA
LVOW05s0717221213

366351LV00004B/11/P

2 370000 134332